Playing the
Harmonica

Playing the
Harmonica

Dave Oliver

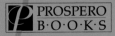

PROSPERO
B·O·O·K·S

This edition produced for Prospero Books,
by arrangement with Haldane Mason Ltd

M 10 9 8 7 6 5 4 3

ISBN: 1-55267-251-4

A HALDANE MASON BOOK
Editor: Ian Kearey
Designer: Rachel Clark
Illustrations: Rachel Clark

Colour reproduction by CK Digital, UK

Printed in China

Picture Acknowledgments

Sylvia Pitcher: 7, 58.
Redferns: James Barron 29, 46–7; Harry Goodwin 15; Mick Hutson 38–9;
Bob King 35; Michael Ochs Archives 9, 18, 50; David Redfern 10, 17, 32, 33, 49;
Ebet Roberts 12; S&G Press Agency 59; Dan Smiley 31.
Courtesy of Hohner: 3, 16, 20, 21, 22, 24, 26, 28, 42, 44, 45, 61.

Contents

Introduction

Let's start by saying that this book is never going to turn you into a Sonny Boy Williamson or a Stevie Wonder – that's not how it works. But it will give you an introduction to the basics of playing and reading music, and with any luck point you in the direction of a fistful of good music.

For such a simple instrument, the harmonica has a rich and varied history, which is still developing today. Once considered a child's toy, it is now the favourite instrument of a range of virtuoso players in all kinds of styles, ranging from blues to rock to jazz to classical, and pretty much everything in between.

But the great thing about the harmonica is that you can take it as far as you want. It's easy to get started, so if you just want to play a few tunes around the home it won't take long. Or you can work till your lips bleed and end up playing in concert halls in front of thousands (just kidding – if your lips are bleeding, you're

doing it wrong). Who knows? You might even be able to get a harmonica on MTV, which is a rare kind of sight these days, but as long as people are still picking up the humble harp, who can say where it's going to end up?

Hopefully this book will encourage you to get all fired up and want to become the best harmonica player you can. It might take you a lifetime, but if you want to do it, here's where you start.

Harmonicas are great because . . .
1. You can pick up and play any time, anywhere.

The Greats

There are too many great harmonica players to have any chance of covering them all in this book. Here are a few, however, spanning a range of styles. Follow these guys and you won't go far wrong.

Little Walter

The undisputed king of blues harp (when it's playing the blues, a harmonica is always called a 'harp'), Marion 'Little Walter' Jacobs is often credited with inventing Chicago blues harp – unadulterated blues played through a microphone and amplifier for a raw, distorted, and extremely loud sound. He was known as a wild one both on and off stage, and executives at Chess Records soon discovered that the man with the super-fast style could only record sometime after 2 a.m. – after he'd finished his club dates and was fuelled up enough on bad liquor to get the requisite fire on tape. By all accounts recording sessions could be stressful affairs – as one musician recalled, 'At the drop of a penny, you would have to fight Walter. He was very confrontational.'

His brief career, which included playing with Muddy Waters and touring with the Rolling Stones in 1964 (he was a big influence on Brian Jones' harmonica playing), was tragically cut short by his violent death in a street fight in 1968. He was 37.

Walter's unique sound relied on two things: his unparalleled virtuosity, and his uncommonly large chromatic harp, which few have been able to master. Playing along to records is difficult with Walter, as he plays in a wide variety of keys, but just listen to any of his recordings and marvel at the possibilities of the instrument.

The boss of Chicago blues harp.

RECOMMENDED RECORDINGS
*His Best: The Chess 50th
Anniversary Collection*
(MCA/Chess)

Dylan in his heyday, with guitar and harmonica.

Bob Dylan

Better known for his distinctive sand-and-glue voice and stream-of-consciousness songwriting style than his harmonica playing, His Bobness is still the most distinctive link between traditional folk and country harmonica and the rock world.

It may seem difficult to imagine now, but back in the sixties Dylan *mattered*, and when he appeared at the Newport Folk Festival in 1965 with an electric band, seemingly cutting off his links with traditional folk, the audience went berserk. Fellow folkie Pete Seeger was allegedly apprehended wielding an axe while attempting to cut the electricity cables running behind the stage.

Dylan continues to record with a harmonica today, but he's probably never used it better than he did on his early folk-influenced material, which is showcased on *The Freewheelin' Bob Dylan*, and on his first three electric albums. These first three albums caused a huge ruckus in their day, and they still sound like nothing else, calling as they do on a range of influences including folk, blues, vaudeville, rock 'n' roll and country.

Dylan is by no means a virtuoso harmonica player, and many have criticized his style for sounding loose and lazy. He rarely plays distinct notes, preferring to slur and slide notes and chords together. He also tends to use the instrument sparingly, but he has an uncanny knack of bringing it in just where it's most needed, enlivening a song at the critical moment with a blast of raw, untrammelled power, or offering a plaintive wail that takes the music places that his gravelly voice cannot reach.

Neil Young

Rock survivor Neil Young has been through many stages, from folk to pop through country, psychedelia and grunge metal, and has written hundreds of songs in a career now in its fourth decade.

Originally from Toronto, Canada, he first made a name for himself in California hippy folk-rockers Buffalo Springfield in the mid-sixties, before going solo in 1968. His early solo albums found him weaving between folk, country and rock influences, often on the same album and indeed, to this day, he tends to veer between the extremes of folk-influenced country ballads and hard rock as well as covering just about everything in between.

Primarily known as a songwriter, he has made a virtue out of stretching a limited amount of technical ability as far as it can go, stressing the importance of the quality of the songwriting. His thin, often strained, voice is generally backed by guitar playing which is free of excessive ornament or distraction – he has a knack of finding an original melody of deceptive simplicity, and he can take a few very common chords and make it sound as if you've never heard them played before.

Not surprisingly, his harmonica playing is most effective on his earlier folk- and country-influenced material. His harmonica style often matches his vocals – wistful, plaintive, and evocative. He often uses it to introduce verses with an echo of the vocal line – very simple, but very effective. A great way to practise can be to try to imitate the melody that a singer is singing.

Neil Young's plaintive harmonica is a staple of his country and folk material.

RECOMMENDED RECORDINGS

After The Gold Rush (Reprise)
Harvest (Reprise)
Tonight's The Night (Reprise)
Decade (Reprise)

Stevie Wonder

'Little' Stevie Wonder first made a name for himself when he was just 11 years old. The little blind boy formerly known as Steveland Morris made his first appearance on Motown Records playing harmonica – it was just the beginning of his talents. For such a little fellow he kicks up quite a noise on 'Fingertips Part 2', the instrumental track that launched him into the public eye in 1962. Over a driving soul revue-style backing he swoops and soars, taking the music down to a quiet, almost conversational level, then tearing it up with an astonishingly confident surge of power.

Stevie's harmonica was a major feature on many (though certainly not all) of his early recordings. In the early seventies his harp took a back seat as he began to explore the possibilities of synthesizers on some of his most audacious recordings: *Talking Book, Innervisions* and *Songs In The Key of Life.*

Though a multi-instrumentalist best known for playing keyboards, he still often includes harmonica in his recordings, and indeed it featured in some of his biggest hits in the eighties, including 'I Just Called To Say I Love You' and 'Ebony And Ivory'. He continues to feature harmonica on his own and other people's records on a regular basis.

Stevie has an extremely melodic style, often playing the lead vocal line as an intro to the song. He's also capable of fast, confident runs on a chromatic harmonica, which gives a distinctive sound. You won't hear him bending many notes, but he always sounds funky, assured and melodic.

Stevie Wonder with chromatic harmonica – note the slide button he presses with his right hand.

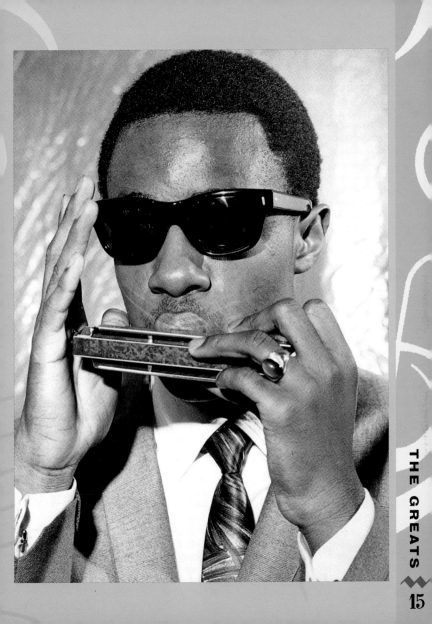

Larry Adler

One of the most respected, longest-playing and most technically proficient of all harmonica players, Larry Adler was born in Baltimore, Maryland, USA, in 1914, but spent much of his career based in England when he was unable to get work at home due to the hysterical McCarthy blacklist, which named him as a Communist sympathizer in 1949.

He is virtually single-handedly responsible for ensuring that the harmonica was treated seriously as a musical instrument in the twentieth century by a white middle-class audience, who tended to respect music only if it was written down. Adler's repertoire spanned jazz, show tunes, film scores (including the Oscar-nominated *Genevieve*) and classical.

He tended to use a chromatic mouth organ (he didn't like the word 'harmonica') for concert recordings, though he could play virtually any variation of the instrument equally well. His style is difficult to define since his range was so broad. He could be plaintive or forceful, play backing or solo – he even accompanied himself on occasion, playing piano with his left hand while he held his mouth organ in his right. But he was always a concise and emotional interpreter of the music, with crystal-clear runs, restrained vibrato and bucketloads of good old-fashioned musicality.

After teaching himself to play the instrument he began performing at age 14. In the thirties he played jazz with legendary Belgian gypsy guitarist Django Rheinhardt, and made his name interpreting the show tunes of jazz composer George Gershwin. He later flirted with classical themes and played with numerous

Larry Adler's 16-hole chromatic mouth organ spans four octaves.

Larry Adler in flight.

symphony orchestras. Up until
his death in 2000 he was still
playing and performing and
had guested in the late nineties
with the likes of Tom Jones
and Sting.

RECOMMENDED RECORDINGS
Harmonica Virtuoso (Mci)
The Best of Larry Adler (Pulse)
Genius of Larry Adler
(Universal/Polygram)

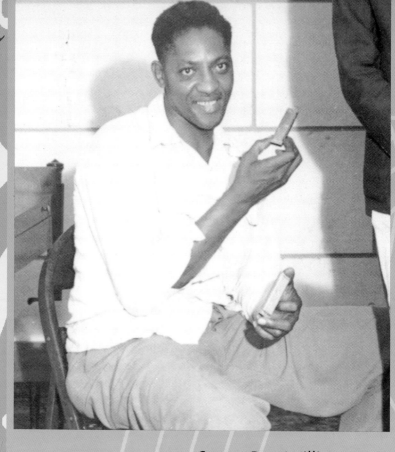

*Country blues master
Sonny Boy Williamson II
(real name 'Rice' Miller).*

Sonny Boy Williamson II

Considered by many to be the boss of country blues harmonica, Sonny Boy Williamson II (real name Aleck Ford 'Rice' Miller) should not be confused with Sonny Boy Williamson I, who was actually younger, but hit fame first. But it was Sonny Boy mark II who really took the harp to its limits. He did party tricks, such as playing the harp while putting it in his mouth lengthways, like a cigar, but he could also blow with fire and tenderness, blues and soul.

One of his chief musical characteristics is his mournful tremolo, a kind of 'ab-waah waa-waa, waa-waa waaah dit/duuu'. He played with acoustic and electric bands, sometimes using a microphone for a distorted electric sound, but usually without. His is one of the most 'vocal' harp sounds you'll hear, with plenty of intense wailing and 'wah-wah'. He doesn't necessarily play loud, but his intensity and commitment mean you always hear him and he always stands out. Also he was never one to overplay, and would often sit out for a period during the course of a record to let the rest of the band come through, which means that when he comes back in with a soaring, swooping single note, it sounds twice as effective as if he'd just been tootling along the whole time.

Born in Mississippi in 1899 or thereabouts, he played the juke joints and fish fries across the South before relocating to Chicago, where he achieved fame on record in the forties and fifties. In the sixties (also in his sixties) he became a star in England and toured Europe with beat blues bands The Yardbirds (featuring Eric Clapton) and The Animals. He contemplated staying in England, even getting himself kitted out in Savile Row suit and bowler hat and a briefcase full of harmonicas, but headed back to Mississippi for his last days, which he spent playing in juke joints until his death from a heart attack in 1965.

History of the Harmonica

The little instrument with a big fan base probably first originated, like many other things, in twelfth-century Indo-China. The simple instrument known as the sheng referred to in seventeenth-century European documents consisted of a gourd with a set of free reeds into which you blew via a series of tubes. We've come a long way, baby.

The first example of the modern harmonica was invented by Friedrich Buschmann in Berlin, Germany in 1821. Aged just 16, he registered a patent for his new instrument, the Mundaoline. This early instrument featured a horizontal range of holes containing reeds, but they could only be blown. It wasn't until the innovation of

Hohner harmonicas were like Bell telephones – they pretty much had the market to themselves for decades, and Hohner is still by far the biggest manufacturer of mouth organs.

Bohemian instrument maker Richter in 1826 that a model featuring ten holes with opposing reeds (one which sounded when blown, another which sounded when sucked) was introduced. His diatonic tuning and ten-hole design was known as the Mundharmonika (German for 'mouth organ').

In 1857, a German clockmaker called Matthias Hohner began to manufacture harmonicas full-time and so began the business which would become the world's largest manufacturer of harmonicas. The company virtually cornered the market, producing a variation for pretty much anyone who might conceivably want one. Many of the harmonicas only differed in terms of the packaging (see the small selection of vintage ones below), but at some time or another, Hohner has produced an example of just about any

Harmonicas are great because . . .
2. There's one to suit every taste.

type of harmonica that has existed anywhere.

All early harmonicas were diatonic, that is they were only designed to play in one key (see page 55 for an explanation of this). Chromatic harmonicas capable of playing all the notes within their range began to be introduced in the 1920s. These harmonicas opened up possibilities for the instrument by allowing it to be used for classical music and the developing music of jazz.

Of course, by this time, the harmonica had already established itself as a popular instrument in American folk music among both the black and white communities. Its ability to convey evocatively both plaintive mourning and good-time jollity has endeared it to generations – helped not least by the ease with which anyone can produce a tune, and its cheapness. Classical players such as Larry Adler and George Fields, and jazz players such as Toots Thielemans, opened up the possibilities of the instrument with recordings of Bach and other elements of the classical repertoire.

In the twenties and thirties the harmonica was a tremendously popular instrument in the developing music of the blues. Hundreds of players were evolving subtle and not-so-subtle variations using this basic rhythm system. The harmonica (or harp in blues parlance, named after some of the earliest American imports, called 'French Harp', even though they were from Germany) proved itself an effective vehicle for emotion.

The blues and folk revivals of the sixties saw the harmonica returning to popular music, with the likes of Bob Dylan, The Rolling Stones and even top boy band The Beatles using it to great effect.

Today the harmonica is less obvious in the pop charts, though it still has a loyal and innovative following of disciples, both reliving its glory years and, of course, helping to develop its next stage in musical history. Are you in?

Types of Harmonica

An instrument with as long a history as the harmonica is bound to have a lot of variety. Over the years there have been many different types of harmonica-style instruments, and there have also been many novelty variations, from Bluebird's giant harmonica, which was produced for promotional purposes in the 1930s, to Hohner's 'Little Lady' – a minute instrument that could be hidden in the palm of the hand and was often used as an accessory in magic tricks.

Today, most harmonicas are one of two types – diatonic and chromatic. Don't be put off by the technical-sounding names, they're still just as easy to make music with.

Hohner's 'Little Lady' miniature harmonica came in many forms.

Diatonic harmonica: top reeds

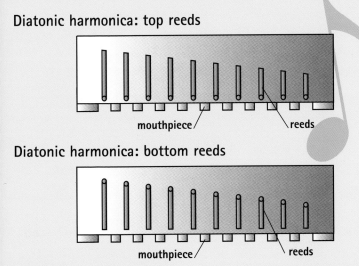

mouthpiece / reeds

Diatonic harmonica: bottom reeds

mouthpiece / reeds

Diatonic harmonica

This is the most popular type of harmonica. 'Diatonic' basically means you can only play notes in one key. You can get them tuned to any key, though the most popular tend to be in C (like the one you're holding), A or E. The great thing is that, providing whoever you're playing with stays in the same key as the harmonica, you can't really go far wrong. Unlike a guitar or piano, which allows you to play any note in any key, the diatonic harmonica only allows you to play the notes in its own key (unless you cheat and bend the notes, but we'll come to that later).

It consists of two brass plates, each of which holds ten brass 'reeds'. The plates are separated by a piece of wood or plastic with ten holes (there are variations in the number of holes, but ten is standard). The whole thing is surrounded by a case with two openings – one that allows air to be blown in from one side, and another that allows air to be drawn in from the opposite side.

Diatonic harmonica: notes

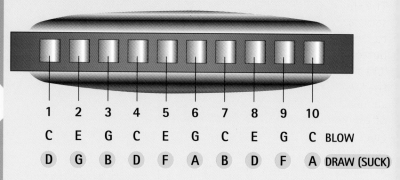

1	2	3	4	5	6	7	8	9	10	
C	E	G	C	E	G	C	E	G	C	BLOW
D	G	B	D	F	A	B	D	F	A	DRAW (SUCK)

Each of the ten holes in a harmonica allows air to be drawn over two reeds, one at the top and one at the bottom of the hole. One of the reeds sounds when you suck, the other when you blow. Each has a slightly different tuning.

Throughout this book, the notes produced when you blow through the harmonica are written as plain numbers:

1   2   3

The notes produced when you draw, or suck, are written as circled numbers:

1   2   3

Chromatic harmonicas with slide buttons.

Chromatic harmonica

The chromatic looks much the same as a diatonic, but tends to be slightly bigger and has a button coming out of one side. 'Chromatic' is a fancy word that really just means that you can play all the notes. Instead of ten holes there are twenty (one on top of the other), but one set of holes is blocked off. When you press the button, it opens the second set of ten holes and closes the first. One set of holes is tuned a half note (also known as a semitone) above the other, so by pressing and releasing the button you can sound all the notes, not just the ones in any given key.

Think of it like this: on a piano you have black keys and white keys. The white keys are the whole notes (A, B, C, D, F and G), the black keys are the semitones, half notes in between the whole notes. So A sharp (written A#) is the same as B flat (B♭), and there are no incidentals (half notes) between B and C and E and F (there are complicated reasons for this but the bottom line is that you don't need to know them – and if you still want to, get some lessons).

If you're in the key of C (like your harmonica is tuned to), all the notes are the same as the white keys on the piano. When you push the button on a chromatic harmonica, you can play the black notes in between.

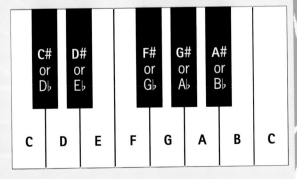

The notes (tones) as they appear on a piano. The white keys are the whole tones, and the black keys are the semitones in between.

C# or D♭ D# or E♭ F# or G♭ G# or A♭ A# or B♭

C D E F G A B C

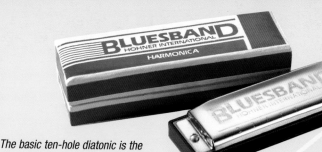

The basic ten-hole diatonic is the most popular type of harmonica.

Which one should I use?

There are good reasons why the diatonic harmonica is the most popular. It's easier to play, it's cheaper, and thousands of people have already used it to make great music. For most popular styles – folk, country, blues, pop – you'll find that there's more than enough in your average ten-hole diatonic harp to keep you busy for a lifetime.

For the more demanding styles of jazz or even classical music, which often require you to jump around between unusual keys, the chromatic is more suitable, although it is a much trickier instrument to master. Even if your heart is in jazz, you're better off starting on a diatonic and moving on to the chromatic once you've got a good handle on the basics.

The bigger harmonicas tend to sound deeper, and the smaller harmonicas, not surprisingly, tend to sound higher. You'll notice that there appear to be a couple of notes missing on your C harmonica – hole 2, for instance, sounds notes E and G, but not the F in between. That's so the harmonica can span three octaves (groups of eight notes, C-D-E-F-G-A-B-C – the second C is essentially the same note, but an octave higher). You can still play those missing notes, but we'll get to that later.

Blues diva Big Mama Thornton works the harp.

Harmonica Styles

People have been playing harmonica all around the world for a century and a half, but nowhere has its effect been more strongly felt than North America. Many of the definitive harmonica playing styles have come out of the US of A, and here are a few of them.

Chicago blues
Little Walter
Howlin' Wolf
Sonny Boy Williamson II
Big Mama Thornton

Country blues
Sonny Boy Williamson I
Sonny Boy Williamson II
Jimmy Reed

Folk blues
Sonny Terry
DeFord Bailey

Blues rock
John Mayall
Paul Butterfield
Lee Brilleaux
 (Doctor Feelgood)

Blues
There are so many different types of harmonica playing, even under the umbrella title of blues. Almost everyone who has made any significant impact on blues harp playing has developed a new sub-genre.

Blues is one of the most accessible harmonica styles to begin with. You can sit in and play along very easily – you can play rhythm or lead to the basic 12-bar blues style, which virtually all musicians are familiar with, and it will still sound pretty good. Despite its simplicity, striving to achieve the heights of some of the masters of blues harmonica, such as Little Walter or Sonny Boy Williamson II, can be a lifetime's work.

Folk/Country

Where blues music is largely based on rhythm, folk and country harmonica tends to focus on the melody. Again, at its most basic level, this can be very simple – just playing simple tunes that are no more complicated than nursery rhymes, but which, in the right company and with the right phrasing, can sound sublime. You can also play accompaniment in Bob Dylan's famous style, which can mean just sounding a single note or chord at just the right moment – easy to practise and a good way to get involved in the music quickly.

Country
Neil Young
Charlie McCoy
Chaim Tannenbaum
Harmonica Frank Floyd

Folk
Willie Atkinson
Rory McLeod
Chris Taylor
Martin Brinsford
Brendan Power
Bob Dylan
Bruce Springsteen
Woody Guthrie

Bruce Springsteen in concert using a harmonica 'rack'.

Pop, Rock and Soul

For a long time Stevie Wonder seemed to have this area all to himself. Pop has the advantage of being free from any pretensions to purity – there's never anyone to say 'that's not real pop' in the way that some misguided 'purists' might comment on blues or folk. Let's not forget, it's all music, it don't matter what you call it, and as legendary jazz man Louis Armstrong said, there are really only two types – good and bad. You decide which one's which.

So pop harmonica is a hybrid of other types of harmonica playing, as well as a whole bunch of new ones. Some people try to make it sound like a saxophone, others like a piano. It can be used as a lead instrument, as a substitute for voice, or as backing. Basically, anything goes.

Pop, Rock and Soul
Stevie Wonder
Brian Jones
  (Rolling Stones)
Paul Jones (Blues Band)
Captain Beefheart
John Lennon
Bob Dylan
Magic Dick (J. Geils Band)

John Lennon often played the harmonica with the Beatles.

Jazz
Toots Thielemans
Tommy Reilly
Max Geldray
Hendrik Meurken
Mike Turk

Classical
George Fields
Larry Adler

Jazz/Classical

These musical styles aren't immediately associated with the harmonica, but there have been a few distinguished contributors. Belgian Toots Thielemans is the boss of jazz harmonica – you may know his playing from the theme tune of the Dustin Hoffman film *Midnight Cowboy*.

New Yorker George Fields has been transcribing and performing the work of Bach

Jazz harmonica maestro Jean Baptiste 'Toots' Thielemans.

for the harmonica for years with some success (although it's unlikely you'll see him on MTV soon). Classical composers such as Brazilian Hector Villa-Lobos and Frenchman Darius Milhaud helped to create the thin but crucial repertoire of written classical music specifically dedicated to the instrument.

Playing Your Harmonica

As you get into playing your harmonica, you'll discover that there are lots of ways to do it. Let's get one thing straight – none of them are wrong, you just have to find what's right for you.

Holding your harmonica

If you're right-handed, it will feel pretty natural to hold your harp in your left hand between thumb and forefinger. Number

Most players hold the harmonica in their left hand, with low notes to the left, high notes to the right.

one hole, the one with the lowest note, should be on the left, and number ten hole, the one with the highest note, should be on the right. This way your right hand is free for cupping over the harp and using wah-wah and muting effects (shown later).

(Incidentally, bluesman Sonny Terry and others do it the other way round, with low notes to the right, but let's get the hang of doing it one way before we try changing things.)

Let's begin with a chord (more than one note played at the same time that sounds good – if it doesn't sound good it's called a dischord, but there's no law against playing them if you want to). Moisten your lips, part your teeth a little and blow into holes 1, 2 and 3. Don't worry too much about getting exactly those holes at this stage.

DON'T BLOW TOO HARD. For one thing, if you haven't broken the harp in yet (see page 60), you could damage it. For another, you'll soon end up out of breath. Concentrate on first blowing, then drawing in your breath in a smooth, relaxed fashion, and try and keep the tone steady and even. If you can do this, it will be invaluable later on.

Brian Jones of the Rolling Stones.

Exercises

Try these basic exercises (plain numbers **1 2 3** are blown, circled numbers **(1) (2) (3)** are drawn):

Exercise 1

1 2 3 (1) (2) (3) 2 3 4 (2) (3) 4 3 4 5 (3) (4) (5) 4 5 6

Exercise 2

4 5 6 (3) (4) (5) 3 4 5 (2) (3) 4 2 3 4 (1) (2) (3) 1 2 3

Exercise 3

3 4 5 (3) (4) (5) 4 5 6 (4) (5) 6 5 6 7 (5) (6) (7) 6 7 8

Exercise 4

6 7 8 (5) (6) (7) 5 6 7 (4) (5) 6 4 5 6 (3) (4) (5) 3 4 5

Remember I said don't worry too much about playing exactly the right holes. Well, you can start worrying now (just kidding, it's easy).

Cover about three holes with your mouth as before and blow. But then try pulling in the sides of your mouth, making your lips form the same shape they would when you're whistling (except that you've got a lump of wood, metal, and plastic in the way, obviously). It'll take a bit of practice, but you'll know when you've contracted enough to sound just one note at a time. Then try moving your lips around so you can blow or draw a single note in any of the holes. Getting better now?

Now let's try some tunes you'll know.

Hot Cross Buns

5 4 4 5 4 4

4 4 4 4 4 4 4

5 4 4

Frère Jacques

4 4 5 4 4 4 5 4

5 5 6 5 5 6

6 6 6 5 5 4

6 6 6 5 5 4

4 3 4 4 3 4

Twinkle, Twinkle Little Star

4 4 6 6 6 6 6

5 5 5 5 4 4 4

6 6 5 5 5 5 4

6 6 5 5 5 5 4

4 4 6 6 6 6 6

5 5 5 5 4 4 4

Alouette

4 4 5 5 4 4 4 5 4 3

4 4 5 5 4 4 4 5 4

Row, Row, Row Your Boat

4 4 4 4 5

5 4 5 5 6

7 7 7 6 6 6 5 5 5 4 4 4

6 5 5 4 4

Three Blind Mice

5 4 4

5 4 4

6 5 5 5

6 5 5 5

6 7 7 7 6 7 7 6 6

6 7 7 7 6 7 7 6 6

6 7 7 7 6 7 7 6 6

5 5 4 4

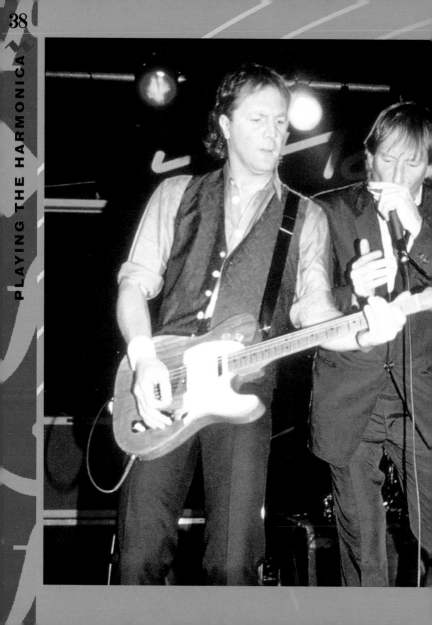

Popular tunes

One of the best ways to get to grips with the harmonica is to play tunes you know. The tunes in this book are old favourites to get you started. But listen to the radio, play some CDs, and try to play the melodies of your favourite songs. If you're into pop or rock, chances are a lot of them are surprisingly easy. But don't just settle for playing them straight – play with them a little, make your own interpretation of them, put them through the blender and see what else you get. Songwriter Elvis Costello once said that the main part of creating songs is trying to copy what someone else has done and getting it wrong. It doesn't matter where you start, it's where you finish that counts.

Lee Brilleaux of English blues rockers Dr Feelgood.

Here are some more tunes to try. The downward arrows in a few of these tunes mean that you need to bend notes – see page 50 to find out how.

Mary Had A Little Lamb

5 4 4 4 5 5 5

4 4 4 5 6 6

5 4 4 4 5 5 5

4 4 5 4 4

12-Bar Blues

2 3 4 5 5 5 4 3

2 3 4 5 5 5 4 3

1 2 3 3 3 3 3 2

2 3 4 5 5 5 4 3

1 2 3 3 1 2 3 3

2 3 4 4 4 4 4 3

Mannish Boy riff

2 4 3 3 2 2 2 2

2 4 3 3 2 2 2 2

Battle Hymn Of The Marines (Halls Of Montezuma)

4 5 6 6 6 6 6 7 6

5 5 6 6 5 4 4

4 5 6 6 6 6 6 7 6

5 5 6 6 5 4 4

7 7 6 5 6 7 6 5 6

7 7 6 5 6 7 6

4 5 6 6 6 6 6 7 6

5 5 6 6 5 4 4

Popeye Theme

5 6 6 6 5 5 6

6 6 5 6 7 6 6

6 6 5 6 7 7 6 6 6 6 5 4

5 6 6 6 5 4 4

Clementine

4 4 4 3 5 5 5 4

4 5 6 6 5 5 5 4

4 5 5 5 5 4 5 4

4 5 4 3 3 4 4

Home on the Range

6 5 5 (4) 5
4 4 4 4 4 4 (3) 4 (4)
3 3 4 (4) 5
4 (3) (3) 5 5 (5)
5 5 5 4 4 (3) 4 4 4

Aura Lee
(Love Me Tender)

6 7 (7) 7 8 (6) 8
7 (7) 6 7 7
6 7 (7) 7 8 (6) 8
7 (7) 6 7 7
8 8 8 8 8 8 8 8
8 (8) 7 8 8
8 8 9 8 (8) 6 8
7 (7) 6 7 7

Oh, Susanna

4 (4) 5 6 6 (6) 6 5 4 (4) 5 5 (4) 4 (4)
4 (4) 5 6 6 (6) 6 5 4 (4) 5 5 (4) 4 4
(5) 5 6 (6) 6 6 6 5 4 (4)
4 (4) 5 6 6 (6) 6 5 4 (4) 5 5 (4) 4 4

Camptown Races

6 6 5 6 6 6 6 5 5 4 5 (4)
6 6 5 6 (6) 6 6 5 (4) 5 (4) 4
4 4 5 6 7 6 (6) 7 6 6
5 6 6 5 5 6 6 (6) 6 5
(4) 4 5 (4) 4

Swanee River

5 (4) 4 5 (4) 4 7 (6) 7
6 5 4 (4)
5 (4) 4 5 (4) 4 7 (6) 7
6 5 4 (4) 4 4
(7) 7 8 6 6 (6) 6 7
7 6 (5) (6) 6
5 (4) 4 5 (4) 4 7 (6) 7
6 5 4 (4) 4 4

Advanced Techniques

Now that you've got the basics, it's time to start playing. Harmonica is one of the most personal instruments – all the greats (and plenty of not-so-greats) sound like no one else when they play.

Tonguing

When you blow or draw, it's not enough to allow the notes to just fade away. That's where your tongue comes in. You use it to 'clip' or 'kill' notes, giving you total control over how they sound.

Try it first on holes 2 and 3. Draw in your breath sharply, and at the same time draw your tongue back and up to the roof of your mouth. If you

find it tricky, try it without the harmonica to begin with. Then try it on the blow chord. It probably won't come first time, but work at it until you can get the 'kill' sharp and exact.

Try it with this train rhythm:

23 **23** 23 23 23 23
23 23 **23** **23** 23 23

Hohner's giant novelty 'Goliath' model had a range twice as great as the average harmonica.

Vibrato

To get this absolutely essential harmonica sound, cup your free hand over the harmonica so that it blocks the air going in and out. Don't worry, you'll never block it completely, but try to create as sealed a chamber as possible. When you move your hand backwards and forwards, you'll notice how the sound changes. Move your hand first from the wrist, then try moving it from the elbow, keeping the wrist straight. Hear the difference in the sound?

Another way to get vibrato (also known as tremolo) is by using your jaw muscles. Drawing in through holes 2 and 3 makes your teeth chatter, like it's a real cold day. You'll find you get a really fast vibrato this way – a pretty cool sound.

Cup your right hand over the back of the harmonica to trap the air, then release it. The movement creates a 'vibrato' sound.

You can get a different vibrato sound by putting your right hand under the harp, covering the back with your two smallest fingers.

Whistling

Once you've got your train going, try adding a whistle sound. Move up to holes 3 and 4 on a blow chord, and at the same time use the vibrato effect. The whistle should be about three or four times as long as the rhythm chords.

The rhythm should finish on a blow chord, which allows you to move on to draw for the whistle.

Like this:

34   **34**

waaaaaah   *waaaaaah*

Then go back to the rhythm.

Teensy weensy harmonica on a string. You never know when it might come in handy.

Hohner's most popular model, the world-famous Marine Band.

Talking

I know, I know, you can do that already. But how it works with harmonica is you make the mouth shapes and move your tongue as if you're talking, but leave the vocal chords out of it – the harmonica's reeds will do that for you. Try saying 'dit' when you draw , or 'dit dit'. It has the natural effect of cutting short the note. And when you blow, say 'dah dah', again cutting off the note a fraction after you've sounded it.

Now try this, again in holes 2 and 3:

23	**23**	**23**	**23**	**23**	23
dah	*dit-*	*dit*	*hah*	*-a-*	*hah*
23	**23**	**23**	23	**23**	23
dah	*dit-*	*dit*	*hah*	*-a-*	*hah*

Blues Harp

Now that you're starting to get the hang of playing your harmonica in the key of C, I've got some bad news. Blues players don't play that way. It's not so bad as it sounds – all you've got to do is learn to play your harmonica in a different key to the one it was built for.

Why

When the blues was being developed by black musicians in the southern states of the USA at the beginning of the last century, they were remembering and interpreting the tonal structures they were familiar with from their African ancestors. This generally meant that some of the notes didn't sound quite like they would in the standard Western notation. To get these effects, which means lowering some of the notes in the scale,

Willie Mae 'Big Mama' Thornton was the first to record 'Hound Dog'. She played a mean harp, too.

you have to 'bend' the notes. Due to the way the harmonica is tuned, you won't be able to get it to sound right if you play it in its natural key.

How
Playing in a different key essentially means starting on a different note (it also means that some of the notes after it will change, but we'll come to that later).

Part of the reason for the success of the blues is its simplicity. It's basically just three notes or chords – and then about a million variations on them.

A basic music scale is like this:

C	D	E	F	G	A	B	C
1	2	3	4	5	6	7	8

You can see there are eight notes in a scale, with the last one sounding the same as the first, but an 'octave' higher. There are all sorts of physics-type reasons for this, but we don't need to go into them here.

The ones we're interested in for the blues are the first, fourth and fifth – C, F and G in the scale of C. But for cross harp (as blues playing is also called), you're starting on a different note, in this case G, so the first, fourth and fifth notes are G, C and D.

Still with us? Don't worry, it gets easier once you start to make the sounds.

Try blowing these notes:

G	G	G	G	C	C	G	G	D	C	G	G
2	2	2	2	4	4	2	2	4	4	2	2

That's a 12-bar blues. You'll notice that there is a sequence of 12 notes. Not all blues sounds exactly like this, of course, but it pretty much all comes from this root, where you start on the first note, move to the fourth, back to the first, then up to fifth briefly, then down to fourth and back to first. You can make the notes longer or shorter, play them as chords, move them around, whatever, but this is your rock, your foundation for building a house of blues.

Little Walter – even in that cardie, he's still just about the coolest blues man who ever lived.

Bending notes

You can really only do this on the draw notes. It's a very tricky thing to do, and it will probably take a lot of practice. But don't worry, anybody can do it once they know how, and once you've got it, you'll wonder how it took you so long. That said, you may be able to get it first time, in which case, good luck!

But for the rest of you, draw in on hole 2. As you do, lower

your jaw and drop your tongue to the bottom of your mouth and back from your teeth. It also helps to narrow the size of your lip opening while you're doing it. Anything happen? Well, try again. And you'll probably need to keep trying. Remember that it takes about twice as much breath to bend a note as it does to sound it straight, so draw hard.

Bending notes is one of the most essential techniques in harmonica playing. It will give your playing style and verve, and ultimately gives you more control. While it's absolutely essential to blues, you can use it for just about any other type of music, including folk, country or pop.

The important thing is not to get discouraged. If you get frustrated, go back to doing some rhythm patterns or basic tunes and come back to it later. It may take days, even weeks, but once you get there

Howlin' Wolf – a big man with one of the scariest blues harp sounds around.

you won't be able to play straight for smiling.

The reason you need to do it is this. When you play straight harp on your harmonica in C, you don't need any half notes (or semitones, as they're called).

The key of C runs like so:

C	D	E	F	G	A	B	C
4	4	5	5	6	6	7	7

However, when you play cross harp, you're technically in the key of G minor:

G	A	B	C	D	E	F	G
2	3	3	4	4	5	5	6

Notice that to get the A, you'll need to bend the note down by a whole tone (two semitones) (see page 55).

Remember that you can only bend notes when you draw on the lower holes (1–5). You can bend on the high holes (8–10) too, even when you blow, but this is even trickier – and to be honest, you won't use them much for blues.

Reading Music

If you want to learn more tunes and you can't do it by ear, you could do a lot worse than learn to read music. It's not essential, but it can come in very useful if you want to check on some notes in a tune that you've heard, but just can't get, or to learn tunes that you haven't heard.

Music is written in the form of dots and lines on a series of five staves. The staves tell you what the note is, and the dots and lines tell you how long to play it for. This diagram shows the range of your harmonica, from 'middle' C (because it's the note in the middle of a piano) to two octaves above middle C.

Note: The arrows indicate a bent note. One arrow means you lower the note by a semitone, and two arrows means you lower it by a whole tone (two semitones).

A basic note is called a crotchet, which counts for one beat of a bar. Other notes are:
  semibreve – 4 beats
  minim – 2 beats
  quaver – ½ beat
  semiquaver – ¼ beat

𝅝	whole note or semibreve	4 beats
𝅗𝅥	half note or minim	2 beats
𝅘𝅥	quarter note or crotchet	1 beat
𝅘𝅥𝅮	eighth note or quaver	½ beat
𝅘𝅥𝅯	sixteenth note or semiquaver	¼ beat

A dot after a note means it lasts half as long again.

𝅗𝅥.	dotted half note or dotted minim	3 beats
𝅘𝅥.	dotted quarter note or crotchet	$1\frac{1}{2}$ beats
𝅘𝅥𝅮.	dotted eighth note or quaver	$\frac{3}{4}$ beat

There are also symbols which show you when not to play, that is, how long to leave a gap.
  minim rest – 2 beats
  crotchet rest – 1 beat
  quaver rest – ½ beat
  semiquaver rest – ¼ beat

▬	semibreve rest	4 beats
▬	minim rest	2 beats
𝄽	crotchet rest	1 beat
𝄾	quaver rest	½ beat
𝄿	semiquaver rest	¼ beat

A bracket reaching across two or more notes means you run the notes together and is called a 'slur' (which has nothing to do with drinking too much whisky).

To help you find the structure of a tune, the notes are divided into 'bars', like so:

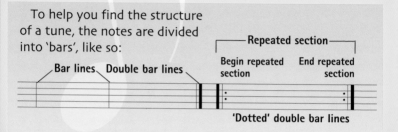

The number of beats that go in each bar never changes once it's set. The way you know is by the time signature. This is two numbers at the beginning of a line of music, and tells you how many beats are in a bar (top number) and what type of beats they are (bottom number).

 Two beats (crotchets) in a bar. Tends to be used for slower tunes.

 Three beats (crotchets) in a bar. This is sometimes called 'waltz time' – all waltzes have that 1, 2, 3 beat.

 Four beats (crotchets) in a bar. The most common time signature in blues, folk, country, rock and pop.

 Six half-beats (quavers) in a bar. It works out to be the same amount of notes as ¾ time, but tends to sound faster and jauntier.

The last things you need to know about are incidentals (sharps and flats). They raise or lower the note by a semitone. The black keys on a piano are all the semitone notes, which come between most of the full notes in a scale. A sharp is written #, and a flat is written ♭. You might see incidentals as a 'key signature' at the start of a piece of written music, like so:

Or you might see them spaced throughout the music next to the individual notes, like this:

Fortunately, your harmonica in C doesn't have any incidentals, just whole tones, so the key signature for C is:

The key signature tells you what key you're in. There are lots of them, and they can get pretty complicated, but the most popular are:

D

E

F

G

A

B♭

Try getting to grips with these tunes:

London Bridge

Swing Low, Sweet Chariot

Good King Wenceslas

4 4 4 4 4 4 3 3 3 3 3 4 4

6 5 5 4 5 4 4 3 3 3 3 4 4

3 3 3 3 4 4 4 6 5 5 4 4 5 4

Jingle Bells

5 5 5 5 5 5 5 6 4 4 5

5 5 5 5 5 5 5 5 5 4 4 5 4 6

5 5 5 5 5 5 5 6 4 4 5

5 5 5 5 5 5 5 5 6 6 5 4 4 4

Playing in Company

With your brand-new harmonica in your hand, no doubt you're raring to go, but take a minute to think about where it's going to take you.

A lot of people forget that there are two ways to play harmonica. You can play solo, in which case you can play whatever you want. Or you can play with other people, either accompanying other instruments or leading them. Once you've got beyond the practising in your bedroom stage, you'll want to get out there and play in front of an audience. And it's even more fun if you've got others to play with. Coming together to make music is one of the oldest social activities in existence. Not for nothing is music a staple of both church and bar-room – basically, it brings people together, and that's how it should be.

Harmonicas are great because . . .
3. Anyone can do it – and you don't need a beard.

Accompanying another instrument, say a guitar or a voice, is a good option – especially when you're starting out. You don't really have to do too much to sound good, and so long as the other musicians are playing in the same key as your harmonica, you won't go out of tune!

The important thing when accompanying is to know when to shut up. Don't wail all over the other instruments just because you can. There's no point in flying off in all directions if the music doesn't make sense as a whole.

Similarly, your playing should be appropriate to the song. Don't go trying any fancy skipping runs if the rest of the guys are trying out a slow, mournful blues tune. And don't hold up the show on a pacy number by laying down a lot of long wailing notes. Just listen – you'll soon get the hang of it, as long as you remember to pay attention.

It really doesn't matter which type of instrument you choose to play with. You can go

When the Rolling Stones started, they were just a few friends playing along to their favourite blues records.

traditional, with a guitar for blues, country or folk. You can accompany straight voice (singing, rapping, whatever). You can jam along with keyboards, beatbox, turntables or violin! It really doesn't matter, just so long as you're making music. And so long as that music sounds good to you, you're on the right track.

Care of Your Harmonica

Look after your harp, and it will give you months, though probably not years, of excellent service. Ignore this chapter, and you'll either spend more than you need to on new harps, or you'll give up, thinking these things just don't last.

Breaking in

The harmonica is a pretty robust little instrument, but take a bit of time to introduce yourself to it.

Don't overstretch your harmonica for the first few days. Blow and draw gently to begin with. This gives the reeds a chance to become accustomed to vibration, without getting all bent out of shape by excessive bending from an overenthusiastic sharp first draw.

Even once it's broken in, be careful to warm up gently, particularly if you happen to be playing in low temperatures.

Cleanliness is next to . . .

The next thing is to keep it clean. Always 'tap it out' on the palm of your hand both before and after playing. This will get rid of most of the gunk that builds up in there (don't worry, even people with clean mouths get dirty harps). After a while it can be a good idea to scrape out the crud that builds up in the opening of the blow and draw holes with a pin – but be very careful not to damage the reeds.

Looking after harp number one

If you've been taking lessons from an old-timer, he or she may advise you to soak your harp in water, turps or even whisky! The best advice is – don't. Yes, doing this can make your harp sound louder, and loosens things up inside, making the instrument easier to play. But it also greatly shortens its working life (much as it will your own, if you soak yourself in at least two of these three substances), and, particularly with wooden harps, the effect of soaking and drying will eventually warp the case – and that means a new harp.

Repair

Chromatic harps can be taken in for repair, and by all means return a harmonica you've just bought if there's something wrong with it. But eventually harps do wear out – notes don't sound so good as they used to, a reed that's got damaged may sound consistently out of tune.

Harps do wear out, so it makes sense to carry a spare.

You may be able to find replacement reed plates if you're very keen, but to be honest, for the price you may as well just buy a new one. Pro players who play pretty strong and hard for a couple of hours most days may expect to get a few months out of a harp, while beginners playing for a few minutes a day without giving it a real workout can expect it to last a whole lot longer. But a harmonica's not for life, so don't sweat it when the time comes to get a new one.

Information

Bibliography and discography
(A few harmonica bibles and discs to get you going)

Books
Blues Harp
Rock Harp
Tony 'Little Sun' Glover
Both by an American session player. Down-to-earth and informative.

Play the Harmonica Well
Douglas Tate and Larry Adler
Essential guide to playing advanced classical and jazz harmonica.

Harmonicas, Harps and Heavy Breathers
Kim Field
The definitive guide to the history of the harmonica and its greatest exponents.

Rock 'n' Blues Harmonica
Jon Gindick
A treasure trove of tips and advice, specially written for people who don't want tips and advice. Includes lessons, songs, stories and a 74-minute 'jamming buddy' CD.

The Pocket Harmonica Songbook
David Harp
Pocket-sized collection of folk, blues and country favourites.

Discography
Compilations
Blues Harp Boogie – 25 Years of Blues Harmonica (Music Club)
Got Harp If You Want It (Crosscut Records)
Blow, Brother, Blow – Charly Blues Masterworks Vol. 32 (Charly)

Little Walter
His Best: The Chess 50th Anniversary Collection (Universal/Chess)

Bob Dylan
The Freewheelin' Bob Dylan (Columbia)
Bringing It All Back Home (Columbia)
Highway 61 Revisited (Columbia)
Blonde On Blonde (Columbia)

Neil Young
After The Gold Rush (Reprise)
Harvest (Reprise)
Tonight's The Night (Reprise)
Decade (Reprise)

Stevie Wonder
The Jazz Soul of Little Stevie Wonder (Motown)
Stevie Wonder's Greatest Hits Vol. 1 (Motown)

Larry Adler
Harmonica Virtuoso (Mci)
The Best of Larry Adler (Pulse)
Genius of Larry Adler (Universal/Polygram)

Sonny Boy Williamson II
The Essential Sonny Boy Williamson II (MCA/Chess)
Sonny Boy Williamson II: His Best (Universal/Chess)

Other titles
The Greatest Songs Of Woody Guthrie (Vanguard)

The Greatest Hits Of Charlie McCoy (Sony)

Jazz Masters: Toots Thielemans (Verve)

Midnight Cowboy (film soundtrack features Toots Thielemans) (EMI)

Springtime in Battersea (Topic)
Tommy Reilly

Internet
Harmonica Lessons
www.harmonicalessons.com
If you don't look at any other harmonica site, make sure you check out this one. Lessons (as you might expect), tips, advice, shop, songs and links a-go-go!

Harpin' On
www.harpinon.demon.co.uk
British site with downloads, info, gear and pretty much everything you need. Even has a jam-along feature that lets you play along in the key of your choice.

Harmonica Country
www.harmonicacountry.com
Hundreds of songs notated for the harmonica – and you can play along, too!

Harmonica Links
www.harmonicalinks.com
Does exactly what it says – around 400 links to choose from.

Harp-L Archives
www.garply.com/archives
The premier news and chat site for harmonicaphiles.

Index of Tunes